Meeting the Challenge

Effective Strategies for Challenging Behaviours in Early Childhood Environments

ECCE 1110

BARBARA KAISER
JUDY SKLAR RASMINSKY

 A project of the Canadian Child Care Federation in partnership with the Canadian Association of Family Resource Programs, the Canadian Institute of Child Health, the Child Welfare League of Canada and Family Service Canada

Meeting the Challenge

EFFECTIVE STRATEGIES FOR CHALLENGING BEHAVIOURS
IN EARLY CHILDHOOD ENVIRONMENTS

Project Manager: Anne Maxwell, Director of Information Services, Canadian Child Care Federation

Authors: Barbara Kaiser and Judy Sklar Rasminsky

Design: Barbara Kaiser and Leographic, Montreal, QC

Photography: Alida Jansen

Cover: Barbara Kaiser

Translation: Diane Archambault

Printing: M.O.M. Printing, Ottawa, ON

Project Advisors:

Kate Andersen, School of Child and Youth Care, University of Victoria, BC; Richard Bass, The Montreal Children's Hospital Westmount Park School Kindergarten Project, Westmount, QC; Doreen Beaton, President, Child Welfare League of Canada, Ottawa, ON; Dr. Joyce Canfield, Department of Psychiatry, The Montreal Children's Hospital, QC; Eleanor Chornoboy, Director, Children's Special Services, Government of Manitoba, Winnipeg; Kathryn Cooper, Canadian Child Care Federation Member Council and Saskatchewan Child Care Association, Regina; David Creighton, Consulting Psychologist, Ministry of Children and Families, Government of British Columbia, Vancouver; Julie Cyr, Garderie éducative Renée Tassé, Ottawa; Dominique D'Abate, Social Worker, CLSC Metro, Montreal; Margaret Fietz, Executive Director, Family Service Canada, Ottawa; Sherry Fournier, Resource Coordinator, Child Care Resources, Sudbury, ON; Chris Gay, Early Childhood Care and Education Consultant, Victoria; Loriana Guiliani, Consultant, Centre de Psychoéducation, Montreal; Leanne

Keffer, Family Services, Government of Manitoba, Winnipeg; Maureen Kellerman, Military Family Resource Programs, Ottawa; Abby Kleinberg-Bassel, Early Childhood and Behaviour Management Consultant, Ville St. Laurent, QC; Cathy McCormack, Early Childhood Consultant, Department of Health and Social Services, Government of Prince Edward Island, Charlottetown; Trudy Norton, Board of Directors, Canadian Child Care Federation, and Director, Burquitlam Child Care Centre, Coquitlam, BC; Avril Pike, Executive Director, Oliver School Centre for Children, Edmonton, AB; Dr. Jalal Shamsie, Director, Institute for the Study of Antisocial Behaviour in Youth, Etobicoke, ON; Alice Taylor, Coordinator, Early Childhood Education Program, Holland College, Charlottetown; Dr. Lee Tidmarsh, Department of Psychiatry, The Montreal Children's Hospital; Dawn Walker, Executive Director, Canadian Institute for Child Health, Ottawa; Pat Wege, Executive Director, Manitoba Child Care Association, Winnipeg

We couldn't have written this booklet without the help of the many dedicated people who so generously shared their time and expertise with us. In addition to our advisors, we would like to thank Dianne Bonozew, Sylvie Bourcier, Barb Coyle, Sharon Hope Irwin, Doreen Jospé, Theo Lax, Jenny Milne-Smith, Lorraine Montpetit and the Quebec Association of Preschool Professional Development, Sarah Mulligan, Robert O'Neill, Tina Roth, Ron Schmidt, Robert Spencler and David Young. Special thanks go to the Henry and Berenice Kaufmann Foundation. We would also like to thank the parents and children of Garderie Narnia in Westmount, QC, whose photographs appear in this book, as well as Narnia educators Mike Bonnell, Giacomo Caligiuri, Basilike Efstathapoulos, Alida Jansen, Dominique Leclerc-Catala, Sonia Maloney, Mary Pallante and Carol Patterson, who have made everything we've written come to life.

For information or copies, contact:
Canadian Child Care Federation
30 Rosemount Avenue, Suite 100, Ottawa, Ontario K1Y 1P4
Telephone: 613-729-5289 or 1-800-858-1412; fax: 613-729-3159
E-mail cccf@sympatico.ca. Visit us on the Internet: www.cfc-efc.ca/cccf
ISBN 0-9685157-1-1
©1999

Contents

Introduction

Did I choose the right profession?

When you were training to work with young children, you probably learned that if you planned appropriate and interesting activities and responded warmly and consistently to the children, you would capture their hearts and minds. If by chance a child pushed, grabbed toys or ignored your instructions, gentle guidance and positive reinforcement would quickly transform her or him into a cooperative member of the group. When you started work, you no doubt discovered that these theories work most of the time, for most of the children.

But once in a while a child appears who turns your world upside down. Let's call him Andrew. He's four years old, with language that's slightly delayed and cognitive and motor skills that so far appear to be developmentally appropriate. Before he came to your centre, he had been to three home care providers and another day care centre.

Andrew's parents said he would be a handful, and he is. By the end of a typical day, he has punched, kicked or sat on almost every child in the group, torn up their pictures and thrown a bucket of Lego across the room — all without provocation or remorse that you can see. He brings out every flaw in your program and taxes every skill you've developed over the years. Yet at the moment he has no diagnosed medical problem, hence no medication, no treatment guidelines and no money for extra staff to help care for him.

You can't manage Andrew's behaviour or prevent him from hurting you or the other children. They no longer feel safe, and they become anxious, lose control, demand attention, copy Andrew's behaviour or are just too scared to do much of anything. You spend your day putting out fires, consoling children and saying no. You know you're not helping Andrew, and what's worse, you don't even like him — a feeling that makes you profoundly uncomfortable. After a while you begin to feel resentful, burned out, inadequate and full of self-doubt. You may even wonder whether you've chosen the right profession.

Someone please throw me a lifeline!

This booklet is a kind of survival manual. Its aim is to give you the information and skills you need to cope with children with challenging behaviours like Andrew. Although research shows that aggressive behaviour in early childhood tends to persist throughout later childhood, adolescence and even adulthood,[1] it also shows that children with challenging behaviours can learn appropriate ways to behave. The adults who work with them and their families can make an enormous difference in their lives.[2]

By helping Andrew, you are also helping the other children — the targets of challenging behaviour, who in Andrew's presence are learning to become victims; and the bystanders, who if they become frightened or excited may act out or even join him.[3] (This is why you sometimes start out with one child with challenging behaviour and end up with five.) When you are prepared — when you know how to handle Andrew's behaviour appropriately, or better still, how to prevent it — the children feel safe, and the challenging behaviour is less severe, less frequent and less contagious. Then it becomes possible to make the commitment that everyone who works with young children wants to be able to make: to welcome and help each child who needs your services.

What is in this book?

This booklet isn't a recipe book or a panacea for all the ills in the early childhood field, and it doesn't come with a money-back guarantee. But it offers ideas and strategies that have been proven to work time and again — and that will work if you give them a chance. There may be weeks between the moment when you first realize that you need help with a child with challenging behaviour and the moment when that help actually arrives. That is the hardest time, the time when you are most liable to burn out — and a time when the strategies here will be useful. But don't wait until then to try them out. They can benefit every child in your setting, not just those with challenging behaviours.

The booklet is divided into two parts. Part I explains the background — some of the theory and research that underlie effective practice. Part II is more practical. It describes strategies for managing challenging behaviours.

It's always hard to try out new methods, especially when they focus on prevention. But the truth of the matter is that prevention is far more efficient and effective than having to deal with challenging behaviour. Whatever you invest in it will save you time, energy and trouble later.

I. The Why and Wherefore

What is challenging behaviour?

Challenging behaviour is any behaviour that:

- interferes with children's learning, development and success at play;
- is harmful to the child, other children or adults;
- puts a child at high risk for later social problems or school failure.[4]

Estimates of the prevalence rate of aggressive and antisocial behaviour among preschool-age children range from 3 to 15 percent.[5]

We have limited our focus to aggressive behaviours, but many of the ideas here work equally well with children who have timid and withdrawn behaviours, which certainly also qualify as challenging.

But isn't this behaviour sometimes appropriate for the child's age?

Human beings are not born with social skills; they learn them. Very small children don't have words to express their feelings and needs. They don't yet connect actions to consequences, they are impulsive and self-centered, and even though they may notice others' feelings, they don't begin to develop the ability to empathize until they are about two years old.[6] They use any means at their disposal to get what they want and to make themselves understood. The National Longitudinal Survey of Children and Youth, a random sample of 22,831 children living in Canada, found that physical aggression starts at about nine months and peaks between 27 and 29 months, when 53.3 percent of boys and 41.1 percent of girls try it out.[7] By about the age of three, most children learn to use alternative, prosocial strategies rather than physical aggression.[8]

A Rose by Any Other Name

Challenging behaviour can be direct (like hitting, pushing, biting, pinching, kicking, spitting or hair-pulling) or indirect (like bullying, teasing, ignoring rules or instructions, spreading rumours, excluding others,[9] name-calling, destroying objects, refusing to share, not paying attention or having temper tantrums). Now we call these behaviours "challenging," but we've also labeled them — or the children who use them — as:

difficult	aggressive
unsociable	violent
antisocial	assaultive
a handful	low threshold
high needs	high impulsive
bad	oppositional
out of control	non-compliant
acting out	mean
hard to manage	problem
at risk	attention-seeking
disruptive	willful

What causes challenging behaviour?

Theories about the origin and development of aggressive behaviour abound. Some emphasize social learning, others cognition, problem-solving or attachment. The only certainty is that the causes of challenging behaviour are extremely complex and intricately interconnected.

However, research does show that certain factors increase a child's risk for developing challenging behaviour. The factors fall into two broad categories, biological and environmental.

Biological risk factors

- *Pregnancy complications, perinatal stress, prematurity, birth trauma and congenital defects* may put children at risk by causing neurological damage.[10]

- *When mothers use drugs, drink alcohol or smoke during pregnancy*, their children are at increased risk for behavioural, cognitive, learning and developmental problems. Babies exposed to cocaine and babies with Fetal Alcohol Syndrome (FAS) or Fetal Alcohol Effects (FAE) may exhibit severe and long-lasting effects.[11]

- *Developmental delays, especially language delays*, are often associated with challenging behaviours. Studies report a 50 percent overlap between language delays and behaviour problems.[12] Sensory integration problems — which include poor motor coordination, hypersensitivity to sensation, distractibility, hyperactivity and slow speech — may also be linked to challenging behaviours.[13]

- *Attention deficit disorder (ADD)* and *attention-deficit hyperactivity disorder (ADHD)* can also contribute to antisocial and violent behaviour.[14] ADD/ADHD is a neurological syndrome whose major symptoms include inattention, impulsivity and sometimes hyperactivity. Now thought to be largely genetic,[15] it isn't usually diagnosed until a child is at least five, although the hyperactive symptoms appear earlier.[16]

- *Temperament* is a significant factor. In 1956 New York University psychiatrists Alexander Thomas and Stella Chess began the first longitudinal study of personality traits and discovered that children are born with distinct temperaments. Thomas and Chess identified three types: easy, difficult and slow to warm up.

  In trying to figure out why only half of the children with difficult temperaments developed emotional or behavioural disturbances, Thomas and Chess evolved the concept of "goodness of fit": serious problems are more likely to arise, they said, when the temperament of the child and the expectations of the parent or caregiver are out of sync. A child's temperament has a major impact on her environment — caregivers included.[17]

- *Gender* plays a part in challenging behaviour, but it's not clear whether this is a matter of biology or environment. In the National Longitudinal Survey, boys rated higher than girls on physical aggression in every age group,[18] but aggressive behaviour in girls is becoming more common.[19]

Environmental risk factors

- *Poverty and the social conditions surrounding it* — poor housing, poor nutrition, parental unemployment, victimization, discrimination — provide fertile ground for challenging behaviours.[20] According to the National Longitudinal Survey, "Boys and girls from the lowest socioeconomic levels clearly had the highest physical aggression scores." They also ranked higher on indirect aggression.[21]

- *Exposure to violence* brings a high risk of challenging behaviour. Children who witness violence at home or who have been physically, emotionally or sexually abused are especially vulnerable.[22]

- *Parenting style and family factors* also figure in the development of challenging behaviours. When one or both parents use arbitrary, harsh, inconsistent, coercive discipline, when they respond negatively and are uninvolved with their children, when they model antisocial ways to resolve disagreements and when they don't supervise their children, the children may respond with defiant, aggressive, impulsive behaviours.[23]

- *Viewing violent television* makes children more aggressive and seduces them into watching even more violent television to justify their increasingly aggressive behaviour.[24]

- *Low quality child care* can put a child at risk. Groups that are too large, spaces that are too small or too big, untrained or too few educators, lack of structure, not enough or too many toys, can all contribute to challenging behaviour. So do too many transitions, too much noise and too many demands on children who aren't developmentally ready to handle them.[25]

Batteries Included

Two books — *The Difficult Child* by Stanley Turecki and Leslie Tonner and *Raising Your Spirited Child* by Mary Sheedy Kurcinka — expanded and popularized Thomas and Chess's work. A difficult — or spirited — child comes endowed with several of the following character traits, which can seem either positive or negative, depending on your point of view:

Activity level: always on the move; active, restless.
Perceptiveness or distractibility: notices everything; difficulty concentrating.
Intensity: powerful reactions; loud whether happy or angry.
Regularity: unpredictable about sleeping, eating, etc.; changeable moods.
Persistence: committed to tasks; stubborn, can't be reasoned with.
Physical sensitivity: responds to the slightest touch, smell, sound, sight, etc.
Adaptability: uncomfortable with transitions and changes in routine.
Approach/withdrawal: withdraws from new situations, people, places, foods, etc.
Mood: serious and analytical; seldom shows pleasure, cranky.

Roughly 20 percent of children have difficult or spirited temperaments. There is no correlation between temperament and intelligence, gender, birth order or social and economic status.[26]

Words Hurt

According to Toronto psychologist Tom Hay, emotional punishment can cause even more developmental problems than minor physical punishment.

Emotional punishment damages the relationship between the punisher and the punished, creates a climate for confrontation, hurts a child's sense of safety and interferes with learning. Children who've been controlled with punishment may learn to use aggression to control others. Punishment can destroy self-esteem by sending the message, "You're bad and you deserve to be punished."

People who work with children agree that physical punishment is never appropriate. But did you know that the following practices are also punitive and unacceptable:

- threatening
- scaring
- humiliating
- yelling
- embarrassing
- annoying
- insulting or putting someone down
- teasing
- intimidating.[28]

Is there any way to protect a child against risk?

Challenging behaviour is not inevitable, even when a child is at high risk. On the contrary, some factors protect children. Researchers refer to this ability to stave off risk as "resilience." Here are some of the factors that enable children to cope well despite adversity:

* an easy temperament;

* problem-solving skills, including the ability to plan;

* sociability;

* skill-based competence;

* self-esteem;

* involvement in hobbies;

* having responsibility.

Families and other people in their lives can increase children's resilience by:

* having high expectations and supporting the child as she tries to extend her reach;

* encouraging the child to participate in activities and to take responsibility;

* being a caring, supportive adult presence (in addition to the parents).

As the National Crime Prevention Council puts it, "An interested, caring adult [like a grandmother, older sibling, teacher, child care provider or coach] can serve as a protective factor for the child by role modeling social competence and by providing support."[29]

The bottom line

No matter which risk factors are present, it is not productive to blame — especially to blame the child, the parents or ourselves. It makes more sense to focus on elements in the child's immediate environment that we can influence directly and to try to boost his capacity to overcome risk. When we work with a child over a period of time, we can help him to develop the skills he needs to function successfully with other people. What we teach him stays with him and protects him in a variety of settings.

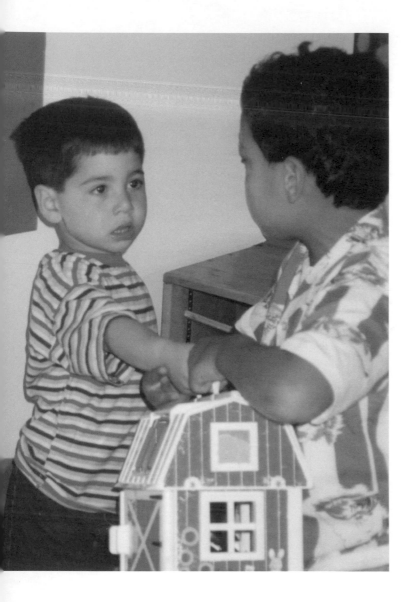

Do children outgrow their challenging behaviour?

Sometimes yes, sometimes no. Studies show that preschool-age children with behavioural problems often turn into difficult school-age children, delinquent teens and violent adults.[30] Richard Tremblay and his colleagues at the University of Montreal found that eight percent of the boys in a low income neighborhood were highly physically aggressive every year from kindergarten to grade 6. On the other hand, another 16 percent who had been aggressive in kindergarten were no longer aggressive in grade 6. The boys with good social skills were less likely to remain aggressive.[31]

What happens to these children if their challenging behaviours continue?

They have poor self-esteem, and they remain at high risk for a prodigious number of problems. Their aggressive behaviour, along with their disregard for others and their tendency to think everyone is against them,[32] leads their peers to reject them; and without friends they have no chance to learn the social skills they need. Because their teachers often don't like them either, and because they find it hard to solve problems, they don't do well at school, and they're likely to be held back or placed in a special class.[33] All of this raises their risk for delinquency, gang membership, substance abuse and psychiatric illness. As adults they are more likely to commit violent crimes.[34] The boys may become batterers, and new research is finding that the girls, who are at risk for early pregnancy and single parenthood, lack parenting skills and may be mothering the next generation of children with challenging behaviours.[35]

What is the role of the brain in this process?

Recently neuroscientists have found that early experience — especially in the first three years — influences the connections within the brain itself. Every experience, positive and negative, has an effect.

A baby is born with 100 billion brain cells, but only a small proportion of them are connected. As she interacts with her environment — eating, crying, gurgling, watching and listening to her parents and caregivers — her brain cells send and receive signals, making 1000 trillion connections by the time she is three. If she uses a connection repeatedly, it is reinforced; if she doesn't use it, it is lost. These connections or networks become the permanent wiring of the brain and allow her to think, learn and behave, both as a child and as an adult.[36] This is where biology and environment, nature and nurture, finally merge.

There are critical periods or "windows" for each of the brain's systems to develop. For example, if the brain isn't exposed to visual stimulation in the first two to three years, the child will never have normal vision.[37] By stimulating different areas of the brain, the quality of care that a child receives affects her capacity to learn, to empathize and to control her emotions and behaviour.[38]

When is the best time to try to change a child's challenging behaviours?

Although there is clear evidence that people can continue to develop throughout their lives, our ability to change reaches its apex in the first decade of life, particularly in the first three years.[39] After that it becomes harder and harder to alter entrenched behaviour patterns. Children with challenging behaviours tend to enter a downward spiral, where each step makes the risks greater.[40]

But we can halt this descent. If we act early and intensively, we can increase children's resilience, diminish risks, bolster self-esteem and help them to learn prosocial behaviours — thereby assisting them to develop new brain networks that will serve them well in the years to come.[41] Because aggressive behaviour is so persistent, it is vitally important to continue to support these children to ensure that they maintain any improvements they've made.[42]

Aren't children with challenging behaviours better off in special settings?

Not usually, though of course it depends on the needs of the individual child. To learn to function in society you must be in society. Children with challenging behaviours desperately need to learn social skills to protect them in the future. Their socially competent peers, who can act as role models and reinforce their attempts at positive behaviour every day, are the best possible teachers (if there are enough properly trained adults around to support them, of course).[43]

The other children are learning, too. They learn how to help a friend, how to stand up for themselves, how not to become victims. Above all, they learn that people are different and that everyone is a valuable individual.

II. The Strategies

Nothing I learned in my training and all my years in the field seems to work with this child!

It may feel that way at times. But it's more likely that when Andrew punches Liane in the stomach for no apparent reason, a lot of what you know flies straight out of your head. Instead of letting panic get the better of you, think about your skills. Then concentrate on fine-tuning them and extending your repertoire.

The caring connection

Your relationship with the children is the most powerful tool you have. As you care for them, you come to learn all about them — their temperaments, developmental levels, play skills, families, cultures. You know what they enjoy, what frightens and frustrates them, what makes them sad or mad. They flourish and their self-esteem soars because you know them well, treat them with respect and honesty, and make them feel special and important.

Current research says that "day-to-day, taken-for-granted social interactions...lay the foundation for the child's development of sense of self, attitudes, values, and behavior patterns." [44]

"Who are you?" said the caterpillar

This crucial relationship may falter when challenging behaviour enters the picture. It requires much more caring, patience and resourcefulness to get past the behaviour, separate it from the child and find the real person underneath. That is why you have to look closely at the second party in this relationship — yourself.

15

Like all human beings, you come equipped with trunkloads of emotional baggage. Normally you can handle it, but a child's challenging behaviour may touch on unresolved issues in your life, and the result is that you're defensive and stressed when you most need to stay rational and in control.

Having these feelings doesn't mean that you're doing a bad job. On the contrary, they provide you with a learning opportunity, warning you to become aware of what pushes your buttons. Children are taking their cues from you all day long, and any strong reaction on your part may frighten them and inhibit learning. It is important to show that you can accept, control and express your feelings in direct and non-aggressive ways; and it is important to show that you aren't afraid of their intense emotions and won't punish, threaten or withdraw from them.[45]

You can't do this when you're out of control yourself. You don't have to practise transcendental meditation, but you might have to make a conscious effort to step back, breathe deeply, count to five or imagine yourself somewhere else. If one of your colleagues relates to a child with challenging behaviour more easily than you do, observe her, talk to her about what she does and try it. Ask yourself, "What would Louise do in this situation?" If you can stay calm enough to respond appropriately, the child will feel safer and the challenging behaviour will probably diminish.

How important is it to prevent challenging behaviour?

Extremely important. Many children use the same challenging behaviour for years because they don't know any other way to behave, and that behaviour becomes firmly entrenched. To break the pattern they need to stop using the behaviour for a very long time. Though a month of appropriate behaviour is a good start, it can't offset three years' worth of inappropriate behaviour. The more we help children refrain from their challenging behaviour, the less they're learning to use it — and the less likely that it's embedding itself in their brains.[46] If you can anticipate when and where the child will have trouble, prevent the situation from occurring, and remind him of what to do instead of waiting for him to make a mistake, you can build a new pattern: the child begins to reap the rewards of appropriate behaviour, feels good about himself and yearns to have that feeling again. As the old saying goes, 28.3 grams of prevention is worth 454 grams of cure!

But sometimes challenging behaviour seems to come out of nowhere

Indeed it does — but it's usually because outrageous behaviour like spitting grabs our attention more readily than subtle signs like hair-twirling. When we look back with the wisdom of hindsight, we can often see that there were earlier signals.

Fortunately there are many ways to intervene early — we can manipulate the physical environment, the program, the social context, change our own approach to the child, and look at things from the child's perspective.

The physical environment

Depending on how it's arranged, the physical environment can elicit either aggressive or prosocial behaviour.

- Too many people in a space — children, staff, volunteers, parents — leads to frustration and aggression. Limit and control the number who can play in each area, depending on the size of the space, the activity, the availability of materials and the chemistry of the children playing.

- Too much open space inspires running, chasing and chaos. Use low bookcases to divide large spaces into uncluttered, well organized areas with different functions like dramatic play, quiet reading or messy play. Lay out clear pathways from one area to another, and make at least two entrances to each so that the children inside will welcome others more readily.[47] (Keep an eagle eye on the dramatic play, woodworking and block areas, where research tells us aggressive behaviour occurs more often.[48]) Group the furniture and materials to encourage children to play together. Seated on either side of a small table, two children can each have their own space — yet share the crayons or paste in the centre.[49]

- Too much noise or loud music makes it hard to concentrate, especially for children with ADD/ADHD, FAS or hearing loss. Some children also find it hard to deal with smells or bright lights and colours. Lower the level of stimulation by leaving some of the wall space blank, turning off the music and putting away some of the toys.

- Too many choices and/or too many toys create confusion — but too few create conflict. Resolving this dilemma requires careful judgment. Very young children will do better if you provide duplicate toys. Older children can share — within reason. You might try doubles at the beginning of the year and gradually replace them with materials that extend the use of your other toys. Choose a wide range so that children with different interests, cultures and developmental levels will all find something to do. (The tactile experiences of sand and play dough are good alternatives for children who have trouble sharing.) The storage space should be well organized, clearly marked and at the children's level so that they can get what they need without your help.

- Competitive games, violent toys and playing violent roles (like superheroes) incite aggressive behaviour. [50]

17

The program

A child with challenging behaviour dares us to examine our schedule and program as well. If Maria wanders around poking people during the rainy-day video, offer a choice of puzzles in another area — or plan a different rainy-day project. When you set up an activity, think not only of the skill you want to teach but also of the behaviour you are trying to encourage.

Look especially at minimizing transitions and waiting times, which are veritable cauldrons of challenging behaviour.[51]

- Children feel more comfortable when they know what's coming next. If you give them a few minutes' warning, they can finish up what they're doing and prepare for the next activity.

- Post a picture schedule to help them understand. If the schedule changes, tell the children in advance and move the pictures appropriately.

- Make the transition fun. Sing songs. Become mice, robots, frogs, airplanes.

- Plan to be the partner of a child who tends to lose self-control during transitions.

- Prepare your materials for the next activity before the children arrive.

Circle and story time are also often problematic. You don't need to eliminate them (though if half your group can't handle them, it would make life a lot easier!), but it's useful to think about whether they go on for too long, whether they're interesting and varied enough, and whether the children get enough opportunities to participate actively. If you have a very fidgety child, let the whole group sit on balls or "sit-and-move" cushions (used by occupational therapists). If you have a child who's easily distracted, seat him facing you with his back to doors and windows. You could even allow a child to play quietly outside the circle if he asks appropriately.

Children who have trouble staying still during quiet activities could work standing up or get materials for the others; children who finish quickly could do additional work or help others. Set up so that they can play in small groups or at learning centres where they don't have to wait as long for a turn.[52]

Children need long periods of uninterrupted play to nourish their creativity and imagination — and to feel satisfied (and willing to share and cooperate).[53] But some need more structure and guidance during free play. Plan carefully and change your presentation — but not your expectations. Give them a limited choice or break activities into smaller bits, and tell them you'll come back in a few minutes to see how they're doing. Instead of forcing the child to fit into the program, help him to learn by bending the program to meet him where his developmental level, individual temperament and culture require.

The social context

The most obvious way to alter the social context is to address the needs of individual children. Give them permanent compatible partners for transitions; assign seats at lunchtime and snack so that Thomas and Chloe, who always fight when they're together, sit at different tables. If you have more than one educator for the group, divide the children into smaller groups to keep those flammable elements apart and to give them the chance to learn from their more socially adept peers.

You can change the social context for everyone by creating rules and policies. Rules for the children are usually based on their primary need, to be safe. Child Care plus+ at the University of Montana mentions three basic ones: respect the rights of others; avoid danger; and take care of the environment (toys, materials, rooms, etc.).[54] Include the rules in your written handouts,

display them prominently, and explain them to new children and parents. Use natural opportunities and activities like story-telling, puppets and role-playing to help the children make them their own. Evaluate them periodically — if they're no longer valid, change or cancel them.

The adults who work in the setting must understand both the rules and the philosophy behind them if they are to enforce them appropriately and consistently. It is the guidance or behaviour management policy that describes how to do this. Make this policy a central part of the orientation for new employees, and discuss and revise it with the whole staff on a regular basis.

Although social skills have long been a staple of early childhood education, you can make an impact on the social context by teaching them proactively. Giving them formal status highlights their value and changes the ambience of the entire program.

Learning social skills is a major developmental task of early childhood, and it has life-long implications. Socially adroit preschoolers make friends and resolve conflicts more readily, are less likely to be rejected or victimized, and are at lower risk for many of the problems that plague their less sociable peers. In other words, their prosocial skills protect them.[55]

In the last few years, a virtual library of user-friendly social skills programs has appeared on the market. Programs like Second Step, developed by the non-profit Committee for Children in Seattle, teach empathy, impulse control, anger management and problem-solving skills using concrete tools like photos,

puppets, stories, dolls and props, along with role-playing and dramatizations. (See Resources, page 39.)

Like anything else you teach, social skills should be developmentally appropriate. It is also important to pay attention to individual differences. The Vancouver-produced video series *Making Friends*, which focuses on peer relationships, gives excellent pointers for evaluating and improving a child's skills. (See Resources, page 39.)

When you're presenting a social skills activity, remember that you're a role model, and concentrate on being your prosocial best. If some children don't want to participate, use their own stuffed animals to engage their interest or let them listen from the playdough table. Disguise and recycle real incidents using puppets, drawings, books, role-playing and discussion. With this impersonal, externalized approach, no one feels picked on and everyone develops skills for the next time.

These tools help the children to understand their feelings and to practise what to say and do in interactions with their peers. When they are applying what they've learned to real situations, your job is to stay closely attuned and to coach, prompt and reinforce to ensure that they get the desired results. Tyrone's angry outbursts made the other children afraid of him, but after the group talked about feelings and played with the feeling puppets, he tried to use words instead of his fists. With the teacher's assistance, the other children understood how hard this was for him and wanted to help. As they became more willing to include him, his social skills and self-esteem improved.

How can I change my approach to the children?

Changing your approach to the children presents the biggest challenge of all, but it is also essential. As psychologist Kevin Leman puts it, "There is no way that you can change anyone else's behaviour. You can only change your own, and when you make a genuine effort to do that, the strangest thing happens. It allows other people in your life to make the behaviour changes that you've been hoping for."[56]

According to WEVAS (Working Effectively with Violent and Aggressive Students), a course written by Manitoba psychologists Neil Butchard and Robert Spencler[57] (see Resources, page 39), in order to prevent challenging behaviour we must start with its very earliest signs, anxiety and agitation.

When children are feeling competent — when their minds, bodies and emotions are in the proper gear and they are functioning well — they are ready to learn. But they can drop out of this competent state at any time. Anxiety is a kind of early warning system that something is amiss, and if it continues it can give way to agitation, aggressive behaviour or even assaultive behaviour. The sooner we can stop this downward slide the better.

The signs of anxiety are subtle — and different in each child. Diane's face turns pink; Paul whines. This is where your strong relationship with the child comes in. When Diane turns pink, you can recognize that she is anxious and respond in the open, caring, understanding way that WEVAS calls "open communication." Here are some examples:

• Use your body language — smile, nod, touch, hug.

• Listen attentively — "who," "what," "where" and "when" questions help the child to tell you what's on her mind.

• Ask "Can I help?" "Can Miranda play with you?" "Do you want to sit with me for a while?" (If the child doesn't want to respond verbally, respect her wishes.)

• Show empathy by validating and paraphrasing what the child is telling you.

• Reframe her statements in a positive light if you can do this honestly ("You're learning something brand new").

• Respond to the need within the child's message.

When we don't respond to their signs of anxiety or our open communication isn't effective, children's behaviour may escalate to agitation. Their reactions grow bigger, they upset other children, and they seem to be losing control — Phillip sucks his thumb harder as he becomes more agitated.

Tell-Tale Signs

We can prevent challenging behaviour by catching it in its earliest phase, anxiety. The signs vary with the child. By knowing her well and watching closely, you can identify these and other signs that indicate what she is feeling (angry, sad, irritable, grouchy, insecure, frightened, frustrated, worried, confused, panicky, etc.).

Physiological: tears, peeing, clenched teeth, pallor, rigidity, rapid breathing, sweating, fidgeting, vomiting

Behaviour: downcast eyes, withdrawing, hair twirling, thumb sucking, hair sucking, clothes sucking, hoarding, clinging, biting fingernails, whining, noisy, quiet, screaming, masturbating, smirking, giggling

The early stages of agitation call for a "teaching response" that makes your expectations clear: "Eric and Sean, during lunch we sit at the table."

If they don't follow your instruction, you may need to use a "limiting response" that will help them to think by giving them a choice and setting a clear limit: "Eric and Sean, you decide: you can sit together or you can sit at different tables."

The first principle of teaching and limiting responses is to be positive: tell the child what to do, not what not to do. In other words, try to delete "stop," "don't" and "no" from your vocabulary (except to keep a child safe in an emergency). Replace these negatives with positive, respectful, non-threatening statements like "Please walk in the hallway."

While you're at it, get rid of "I need you to..." and "you need to..." Children don't care what you need, and it's presumptuous to tell them what they need. Everyone understands better when your statements are straightforward. Eliminate "Why did you do that?" too. The child doesn't really know why he did it.

A limiting response helps the child in an agitated state to think about what he's doing in a rational way. You are reminding him that he has choices, the choices have consequences, and the decision is his. Here are some hints for framing an effective limiting response:

• Think about what you're going to say, and make your statement short and specific.

• State the positive first.

• Make both the words and the delivery of the message calm and non-threatening.

• Pose choices that give the child control over the situation.

• Be sure you can enforce the choices.

• Establish the consequences ahead of time and make them fair and reasonable.

• Use language that empowers the child: "I know that you can play with that toy quietly."

• Set limits based on values shared by everyone in the group (for example, everyone should be safe). Help children to identify these values by discussing them together.

• Model the behaviour that you expect. If he must sit on a chair to eat lunch, you'd better sit on one, too.

• Give the limiting response just once. The child's choice will indicate your next move.

• Allow the child time to think about what he wants to do.

• Follow through on the limit you've set.

• Be consistent. The limit is clearer when caregivers agree about when, where and how to apply it.

• Allow for face-saving. If he does what you ask, it doesn't matter if he scowls or does the task begrudgingly.

• Recognize the child's feelings. "I know that this feels unfair to you. We can talk about it later." When the child returns to a rational state, hold the promised discussion.

• Be respectful of the child and of yourself.

Even if the child behaves exactly the same way the next day (and the day after), don't lose heart. Every new situation brings new problems. If the child needs your directions again, give them without anger or resentment. Repetition is normal and essential — he is young, he forgets and he needs to practise.

The world through the child's eyes

You can also head off challenging behaviour by figuring out what the child is getting from it. Enter the early childhood professional as detective. You and everyone else who works with the child must become a team of sleuths working together to solve this case. Fortunately, the child will provide plenty of clues. The key is to see it from his point of view.[58]

Every challenging behaviour can be thought of as a child's solution to a problem[59] and a form of communication. These ideas go back to Plato, who pointed out that a crying baby's behaviour is serving a function — he is trying to get someone to care for him.[60]

This is the underlying principle of functional assessment, a method that behavioural psychologists developed in the early 1980s in work with persons with developmental disabilities. Because functional assessment is so successful, it is now frequently required in the United States whenever behaviour is dangerous or interferes with learning.[61]

Functional assessment is also a wonderful tool to use with children with challenging behaviours.[62] Remember how random Andrew's behaviour seemed? But challenging behaviour isn't really random. Functional assessment helps us to understand where it is coming from, why it is happening at a particular time in a particular place,[63] and the function (or functions) it serves for the child.[64] Even if the behaviour is unacceptable, the function seldom is. Once we understand the function, we can design a strategy to help the child achieve it appropriately.

How can I figure out the function of the behaviour?

Functional assessment asks us to look at the ordinary environment in a special way. In your training days you probably called this method an A-B-C analysis.[65]

A is for Antecedents — events that take place right before the challenging behaviour and seem to trigger it. The research literature mentions demands, requests, difficult tasks, transitions, interruptions and being left alone.[66] Peers' actions can be antecedents, too — think of teasing, bullying, showing off, coming too close or being left out.

It is often hard to distinguish between antecedents and their more distant relations — known as "setting events" — which occur before or around the antecedents. Setting events make the child more susceptible to the antecedents and the challenging behaviour more likely.[67] The number of children in the group, the set-up of the room, the noise level, the type of activity and the time of day can all act as setting events. So can the child's physical or emotional state — being hungry, tired or sick; or being forbidden to bring a favourite toy to the resource program. Setting events are more difficult to pin down or just plain unknowable and often depend on information supplied by someone else — like the mother who remarks that the morning at home was a complete disaster. They may also be impossible to change. (Remember that there are antecedents and setting events for appropriate behaviours, too!)

B is for Behaviour, described so clearly and specifically that anyone can recognize it (not "Samantha is aggressive" but "Samantha kicks other people's legs").

C stands for Consequences — that is, what happens after the challenging behaviour? Do you turn your back on Samantha, reprimand her, put her beside you, look her in the eye, redirect her to the sand table? Does Jean-Marc giggle? Does Samantha end up with Terry's tricycle? Any of these may reinforce Samantha's kicking.

Taken together, the A-B-C's and setting events point you toward the function of the challenging behaviour. Functional assessment postulates three possible functions:

- The child gets something (attention from an adult or a peer, access to an object or an activity). Whether you reprimand her or put her on your lap, Samantha is getting your attention.

- The child avoids or escapes from something (unwelcome requests, difficult tasks, activities, contacts). Ronnie, who is clumsy at gross motor activities, pushes his classmates in the gym. His teacher removes him to the sidelines — and he doesn't have to do somersaults or play catch.

- The child changes the level of stimulation (each of us tries to maintain our own comfortable level of stimulation, and we react when we get too much or too little).[68] Overstimulated by the small, busy cloakroom, Eloise pushes her neighbor against the cubby so hard that everyone hears the thud of his head against the wall, and the whole room goes quiet.

How do I get the information I need to do a functional assessment?

To come up with a hypothesis — a tentative theory — about the function of the challenging behaviour, you will need current and accurate data, preferably from more than one source.[69]

When everyone who works with the child participates, it's easier to figure things out. Begin with a brainstorming session that will prod memories and stimulate thought, and continue to meet and share ideas as often as you can. Teamwork and consistency are extremely important in dealing with challenging behaviour.

Some information is no doubt hiding in your health records, incident reports, daily logs and files — like notes on how well (or how badly) last year's behaviour management plan worked for Elizabeth.

Talk with the parents. Explain what you are doing, and ask if they will share their considerable knowledge and insight in an interview with you. You can also interview people who've worked with the child in the past, including yourself and others on your team, either individually or as a group.[70] Take the questions from existing questionnaires (see Resources, page 39) or make them up yourself. The idea is to put what you know into a systematic framework.

Ask about the A-B-C's and setting events. Which circumstances almost always surround this child's challenging behaviour and which never do?[71] What is the child getting from the challenging behaviour? When does he behave appropriately?[72] You'll want to know what engages him, whether he feels comfortable in structured settings or small groups, where his talents lie. This knowledge will give you direction as you prepare an intervention plan.

By far the best way to learn about a child's behaviour is to observe and collect data about it.[73] We know this seems next to impossible when you're working with the children, but the more you try, the easier it will become. As the great New York Yankee catcher Yogi Berra once said, "You can observe a lot just by watching."

There are two reasons to observe. One is traditional: with data you can measure change reliably. The second is to enable you to see the relationship between the environment and the challenging behaviour.[74]

If you use a video camera in your setting often enough for the children to feel comfortable with it, you could observe the child by videotaping him. You could also ask the director of your program to arrange for one of your colleagues to observe your group, to observe herself, or to call in a consultant. But outsiders can make you nervous, distract the children and change the environment. You, the people who spend time with the children, are actually the most desirable data collectors.[75] Make a chart with spaces for the child's name, the date, time and place, spaces for the A-B-C's and setting events, a space for your hypothesis about the function of the challenging behaviour and a space for appropriate behaviours. (See page 40 for a sample chart.)

As you run your program and interact with the children, keep your eyes and ears wide open. This is when you do the serious work of observing — by paying close attention to what happened just before the challenging behaviour, who was nearby, what happened next.[76] When you have a moment (at lunch, nap, the end of the day), make notes so that your observations aren't lost or muddled. Write directly onto the chart (you can keep it on a clipboard stashed in a convenient spot), or use note cards or post-its that fit in your pocket and transfer your notes later. Others who work with the child should record their impressions, too. Initial the entries so that you'll know who made them.

Collect data until a clear pattern emerges and you know whether your hypothesis is right or wrong or your observations suggest other hypotheses. This usually takes at least 15 to 20 incidents over two to five days.[77] If you've made a substantial effort and things still aren't clear, try to find a different way to observe or bring in additional help.

The most daunting part of this process is not recording the data but watching yourself. You are not merely observing the child's behaviour; you are also observing your own. The challenge is to stay aware of it and record it accurately — without judging it.

What do I do with all this data?

Call the team together for another brainstorming session. It's time to make a plan! When you examine your data, you'll probably see some patterns that clarify your hypothesis about the function (or functions) of the behaviour.[78] For example, what does Andrew get by punching Liane? The team's observations reveal that he often attacks during clean-up and that both children like to be the teacher's partner. Liane often gets this plum position, but when Andrew hits her, the educator removes him from the fray by taking his hand. Punching Liane serves a function for Andrew: he gets the teacher's attention.

Once you've identified the possible functions, the next step is to create a strategy that achieves the same purpose for the child. The ultimate objective is to teach him how to get what he wants by using appropriate means.[79] There are three ways to do this, and you can consider using them all.[80]

Change the environment so that the child won't need the challenging behaviour.[81] Once again, prevention is the best method! Begin with the setting events if you can. Andrew's mother has mentioned that he's not hungry at 6:30 a.m. The team realizes that he will probably have more self-control if he eats something, and they decide to give him a snack when he arrives.

The next step is to change the antecedents. This usually involves changing the physical set-up or the program (see pages 17-18). Because Andrew has difficulty at clean-up, the team members decide to reorganize the shelves and to indicate more clearly where the toys belong. In addition, they will give the children a three-minute warning that playtime is ending and assign specific achievable tasks. The educator will be sure that Andrew gets a task that he likes, and she will help him to finish it. When he has cleaned up successfully, she will become his partner for the transition to snack, and he'll achieve his goal — having her attention — without hitting.

The team hypothesizes that Eloise, who pushed her neighbor into the cloakroom wall, has too much stimulation. They decide that she will put on her outdoor clothes in the peaceful hallway within sight of the educators and the rest of the group in the cloakroom. She, too, achieves her goal of less stimulation without challenging behaviour. She dresses without a fuss, receives lots of positive reinforcement and feels proud to be the first one ready.

Replace the challenging behaviour with appropriate behaviour that achieves the same outcome for the child more quickly and with less effort.[82] By showing Andrew that he can get attention by cleaning up, the team has given him a replacement behaviour. But he may need even more attention. The team decides to concentrate on prompting him to ask for help when he needs it ("If you want me to do a puzzle with you, ask me") and giving him lots of attention when he's behaving appropriately. Because he likes puzzles, they will join him at the puzzle table where they know they can give him positive attention.

Changing the antecedents and finding a replacement behaviour are both more difficult when you've figured out that the child is trying to avoid something. You will probably have to use a variety of tactics and teach new skills, social or physical, even if the child isn't keen to learn them. The team realizes that it's important not to allow Ronnie to escape entirely from gross motor activities, where he really needs help, but they decide to teach him to ask for breaks so that he'll have an appropriate way to escape.[83]

At the same time they will give him easier tasks in the gym, encourage all his attempts, keep the sessions very short, and let him choose a different kind of activity when he's finished.[84] They know that gym is going to be hard for him for a long time, and they must continue to support him. One staffer volunteers to find activities that teach body awareness to improve his competence and self-esteem so that he has more fun playing and is more willing to try.

Ignore the challenging behaviour as much as possible. The idea here is to show the child that the challenging behaviour will not serve the function it used to — it will no longer get him what he wants.[85] The educators decide that if Andrew refuses to take part in clean-up, they will ignore this behaviour and focus on the children who are participating. But whenever he picks up a toy and puts it on the table — whether he intends to clean up or not — they will quickly thank him for helping.

They realize that they cannot ignore his challenging behaviour if someone can get hurt. If Andrew hits, they plan to do the next best thing — limit the attention they give him by attending to the victim, curtailing eye contact and physical contact with him and saying as little as possible.[86] If this doesn't work and his behaviour seems to be escalating, they will use their emergency plan for dangerous situations. (See page 29.)

After long discussion, it becomes clear that ignoring Andrew's challenging behaviour isn't the most efficient way to change it — and they don't want to risk hurting the other children. Instead they will concentrate on changing the antecedents and teaching Andrew replacement behaviours.

After you put your plan into effect, things may get worse to begin with,[87] but they should improve before too long. Assess the child's progress at a team meeting. One way to measure is to count the

occurrences of challenging behaviour (which should have diminished). Another is to notice increases in positive behaviour, such as when the child:

• Initiates private time;

• allows another child to play with him;

• participates in small groups;

• needs the staff less;

• has a friend;

• uses words to ask for help or breaks more often;

• copes better with transitions;

• doesn't hit when he could have.[88]

Even very small improvements indicate that you're on the right track.

If you notice no progress at all, you may need to go back to your data to look for a new hypothesis, new strategies or a totally different slant. Doing a functional assessment is an ongoing, cyclical process where you are constantly trying things out, getting new information and revising your strategies.

What if positive reinforcement makes the child's behaviour more outrageous?

Positive reinforcement is extremely important, but with some children it seems to have exactly the opposite effect from what you expect. At the first kind word they throw games on the floor or kick the nearest person. In the face of such behaviour, it is tempting to conclude that positive reinforcement is the last thing they need.

Not true. Children like this need more encouragement, not less. Their behaviour is telling you that they rarely receive positive reinforcement, and it makes them extremely uncomfortable. If their negative self-image is too strong, they will try to get you to treat them the way everyone else does — negatively — because in their own eyes they couldn't possibly be worthy of your positive attention.[91]

You may notice that when Andrew behaves appropriately, you are so relieved that you almost tiptoe away. You see his positive behaviour as a chance to take a breath or be with the other children. On the other hand, you have eyes in the back of your head when it comes to his inappropriate behaviour. The result? Most of your interactions with him are negative. When a child gets no positive feedback all day, he learns that he can't play or join in. This state of affairs severely damages self-esteem and makes it difficult for him to succeed in the future.

Combating the child's negative view of himself takes commitment, patience and perseverance. It requires you to trust, respect and care for the child so that he can learn to trust, respect and care for himself. Each day create positive moments with him, playing at something he enjoys and telling him you like playing with him. Include other children when you can. Gradually you will increase his comfort zone and accustom him to feeling better about himself and less anxious when he is behaving appropriately.

It is equally imperative to give him positive reinforcement for his spontaneous appropriate behaviours — or even his pauses in challenging behaviour.[92] But be sure to choose the right kind. For some children too much enthusiasm is overstimulating — they prefer their positive reinforcement in small, low-key doses. Body language is a very powerful reinforcer, but many children with challenging behaviour don't like to be touched, so give them a wink, a smile, a nod or a thumbs up instead. Other children may respond well to a pat on the arm, a high five, a head-rub, sitting on your lap or holding your hand.

Is it fair to treat a child with challenging behaviour differently from everyone else?

We're all the same, yet we're all different. Some children need more individualized support than others in order to learn.[93] It is only fair to give them the chance. Children understand this very well. Because they know that Norie has trouble during transitions, they don't mind if she always holds your hand on the way to the bathroom or sits beside you at lunch.

It's easy to confuse being fair with being consistent. The same rules apply to all the children, so any child who hurts another will learn that he is breaking a rule. But every child has different needs, and every child deserves the treatment that is appropriate for her, which means that you may respond one way to Andrew and another to Norie. (If you've done a functional assessment, you've already planned what you'll do — and everyone on the staff will do the same thing, i.e., you'll be consistent.) With Norie it's a good idea to know where she is and what she's doing at all times. She isn't getting anything extra; she's just getting what she needs. That is fair — both for her and for the other children.

What do I do when a child loses control completely?

Despite our best efforts, we sometimes find ourselves face to face with a child who is out of control — in WEVAS terms, aggressive and assaultive. Brian hurls a chair across the room, refuses to listen and kicks you on the shins as you try to move him. He is like a frightened animal in a trap. This problem cries out for a fresh solution — one that permits you to work safely.[94]

The very first order of business is to activate your emergency plan so that Brian will never hurt anyone in the program again. If you don't have a plan, create one now. The most effective way to keep the children safe is to move them out of harm's way. Decide where to take them, arrange a system to alert the whole staff (including a signal like "Code Red") and assign tasks: who will attend to Brian; who will take responsibility for the other children; who will remove the chairs (or other objects that Brian throws); who will talk to arriving parents. The same person can do more than one task — the point is for every staffer to know exactly what to do.

If you're a family caregiver alone with several children, you can plan to stay with the one who's out of control while a capable older child takes the younger children into another room within your sight. Explain the plan to the children and practise it with them when they're in a competent state.

Review the plan periodically to ensure that it's ready to go at a moment's notice.

Reasoning doesn't work

Because Brian is being driven by emotion, reasoning with him doesn't work. Words seem to fuel the emotion, like gas on a fire. When Brian calms down, you can use words to help him return to a more normal state. (A by-product of this approach is that he learns that he can calm himself.)

- *Stay a safe distance from Brian*, both for his sake and for yours, but remain close enough to show that you are attending to him.

- *Distance yourself psychologically*, and relax your face (even if your stomach is in knots).

- *Do not confront him* with your hands on your hips or make yourself big and intimidating. You will just make him feel smaller and defensive and increase the possibility that he'll lash out, especially if his reaction is based on fear. Instead of facing him head on, assume an L-stance, standing sideways, head up, body relaxed, knees slightly bent, to minimize the threat that you pose and to allow him to save face and not to feel trapped. Keep your weight on the foot closest to the child so that you can move away if necessary.

- *Do not try to move him*. If you do, his behaviour will probably escalate. There are two exceptions to this rule. The first is when children are fighting and someone is likely to get hurt. Try hockey referee tactics — wait for a lull in the action, then step in and pull them apart. The second exception is when a child is in danger — if he's running into the street, you have to act.

- *Be aware of your eye contact*, which is critical when a child is in an irrational state. Although it helps some children to collect themselves, it can also ignite the situation, intensify a power struggle or reinforce a child whose goal is to get your attention. Gaze over Brian's shoulder or at the middle of his body. This will help you to keep your face relaxed and your mind clear. When he is quieter, gradually bring your eyes to his to see if he's ready to begin interaction with you again.

- *Do not talk until he is ready to listen*. Try a few short words when he is calm.

- *Do not insist that the child apologize or give a reason for his challenging behaviour*. He doesn't know why he threw the chair, and asking him to say he's sorry gives him attention, encourages him to say words he might not mean, and suggests that it's all right to hurt someone as long as he apologizes afterwards.[95]

When he's calm, spend some private time with him. Each child needs something different, but you could help him to name his feelings ("You must have been pretty angry") and to distinguish between feelings and actions ("It's okay to feel angry, but it's not okay to throw chairs"). Talk with him about other behaviours that might have been more appropriate, and let him know that you still care about him.

He will need your help to reintegrate into the group and to ensure that he doesn't blow up again right away. Stay with him until he feels comfortable.

Whatever happened to time-out?

The early childhood community has been debating time-out for years. The practice has often been misused, and there has even been talk of banning it.[96]

Adherents maintain that time-out tells the child that you care and want to help him keep himself in control. They also believe that time-out interrupts and prevents aggressive behaviour and allows aggressor, victim and adult time to compose themselves without giving undue attention to the aggressor. The yea-sayers say that time-out works because it can be used consistently.[97]

Opponents argue that time-out damages self-esteem by punishing, embarrassing and humiliating the child in front of his peers. In effect it says, "I don't want you here." Techniques that preserve self-esteem are much more effective in the long run. In addition, adversaries say that time-out may worsen the problem or create a new one by increasing the child's anger or anxiety. If she forces the caregiver to spend several minutes getting her into time-out, she gets the spotlight — which may be exactly what she wants. No one remembers the reason for the time-out, and the other children discover an excellent way to capture the caregiver's attention.[98]

Interestingly enough, some of time-out's staunchest foes believe in "cool down," "take a break," "time away," "private time" or "sit and watch." This is because the two sides agree on time-out's goals:

- to give everyone a chance to regain control in a safe place so that when the child re-enters the group she is capable of success;

- to teach children to recognize when their emotions are building to a dangerous level and to recognize when they are ready to function again;

- to allow the rest of the group to continue its activities.

They also agree that to be effective the adult must be calm and respectful, not angry or threatening.[99]

However, these strategies are really much more valuable — and not at all punitive — when you use them preventively. They are a kind of redirection, a way to teach impulse control. When the child feels herself becoming anxious or agitated, she can learn to move away, take a deep breath, close her eyes, do a puzzle, string beads. This self-directed change in locale, activity or stimulation level allows her to settle her feelings, just as jogging or having a cup of tea calms and restores us when we're struggling with a problem. She can return to the group whenever she's ready, knowing you'll welcome her warmly. You can suggest she take a break to begin with, but the ultimate goal is for her to figure out when to do this herself.[100]

What about using restraint?

When a child is dangerously out of control, our instinct may be to restrain him to keep him from hurting himself and others.

There are compelling reasons not to do this. In many provinces, you must get permission from the parents, a physician or the child care authorities before you can restrain a child. You must also have proper training — used incorrectly, restraint can injure both the child and the adult.[101] Restraint is intrusive and punitive; and it doesn't teach a child to calm himself or to meet his own needs. Some children, particularly those who have been abused, may have extreme escalations in behaviour or suddenly become limp and unresponsive when they're restrained.[102] Others actually like — and seek out — the feeling of deep pressure that they get from being restrained.[103] It is obviously better to teach them to ask for a hug and to hold them when they're behaving appropriately.

If you feel the need to use restraint in an early childhood setting, you may be dealing with a child who requires professional evaluation.[104] In any case, it is important to learn self-protective strategies, including how to release yourself safely from holds, bites and hair-pulling.

How can I empower the other children?

Children who are on the receiving end of aggressive behaviour are at risk of more than physical injury. Children who can't stand up for themselves are at risk of becoming targets, and if we solve their problems for them they may learn helplessness and dependency. They may also suffer from the rejection of their peers, depression and impaired self-esteem. Because they may retaliate or launch preemptive strikes against their aggressors, they are even in danger of behaving aggressively themselves.[105]

If they can respond assertively to aggressive behaviour, they gain confidence and self-esteem and show their attacker that they are not victims. But responding assertively is not easy. Help the children you work with by modelling assertiveness and by teaching it both in your social skills program and whenever one child hurts another. When Suzanne says, "Jody hit me," that is your cue to teach: "No one is allowed to hurt you. Did you tell her to stop?" If Suzanne needs more assistance, accompany her to the scene and give her a script. ("Say, 'I don't like it when you hit me. It hurts.'") In this way you teach Suzanne (and the other children) the value of an assertive response and remind Jody of the rules without giving her any direct attention.

Taking a Stand

Encourage children to use these assertive responses — immediately, directly and firmly — to avoid becoming victims.

- To physical attack, "I don't like it when you hit," "Stop kicking me; that hurts."

- To a seizure of objects or territory, "I'm not done with that," "I'm staying here."

- To verbal abuse or discrimination, "Of course girls can play ."

- To unfair treatment, "It's my turn now."

- To teasing or provocative behaviour, walk or turn away.[106]

When is it time to have intervention?

Asking for help is not a sign of weakness. On the contrary: it is a sign of wisdom. You are trying to solve your problem by thinking creatively and acquiring new skills. The crucial thing is to act long before you feel yourself approaching the breaking point. It may take months for help to arrive, and a burned-out adult is not capable of dealing objectively with either the child or the challenging behaviour. At that point you'll barely hear the advice of an expert consultant, let alone utilize it.

To give yourself credibility (and a reality check), collect some data. Remember the observation techniques on page 25. How often does the challenging behaviour occur? How long does it last? How intense or destructive is it? When you observe systematically, you may discover that Jessica is pinching other children just once a day — not every 10 minutes! Then trust your professional judgment — your knowledge of developmental norms, the instinct that you've developed over years of working with children, your awareness of how a particular child can get to you — and seek advice and support from your colleagues or supervisor.

One excellent way to do this is to organize a home-grown mutual support and professional development system. At every staff meeting set aside time for a non-judgmental brainstorming session about problem behaviours, with a different staffer presenting a behaviour at each meeting. The behaviour can be one that's causing trouble or simply one that someone wants to share. (Anything from not sitting for circle to hitting someone over the head with a truck is fair game.) With such an arrangement, there is no finger-pointing. Rather the group recognizes that some children are harder to teach, that everyone needs an outlet and peer support and that people have different perspectives and skills and can help one another.

When in-house methods aren't solving the problem, it is time to call in the experts. At the supervisor's request, a consultant can observe you and the children and give the whole staff some special in-service training. In some areas, this assistance may be as close as the phone. In others, the centre or agency must find both the expert and the money to pay her.

Tell the expert about any patterns you've discovered in the child's behaviour and any strategies that work (even if they work only part of the time!). Your help is critical to her understanding of the child.[107]

Parents as partners

Parents are partners in any program for children. The more closely you work with them, the better.

It is the parents' right to know about any problem with their child as soon as you become aware of its existence, and their assistance is invaluable. They know their child best; they can fill in gaps in the picture; and if they're willing, they can make big strides with the child by working with him at home.

When you meet with parents, you'll need great sensitivity and your very best people skills. Arrange a time that is convenient for everyone — the parents, the caregiver and the supervisor. Be calm, factual, specific and objective. Describe the skills you're working on, the expectations for the group, your guidance and encouragement techniques. Let the parents know where their child is succeeding and where he's having difficulty. Tell them what you see rather than what you think.

Acknowledge that they are experts when it comes to their child and ask for their help. Is any of this happening at home? Have there been any new stresses or changes in routine? What was he like as a baby? What works for them? How can you work together?

Even if they have already identified a problem, any remarks that sound like criticism of their child may cut them deeply. They are doing their best for him, and they may feel upset, defensive or angry. These are all normal coping mechanisms. Try to see things from their point of view rather than passing judgment. Let them vent their feelings, and give them time to come to terms with what you're saying. If they reply that their child's behaviour is no problem at home, politely say that it is a problem in your setting, where he must share space, toys and attention, and you would like their help in dealing with it.

When you talk with any parent, listen carefully to both the surface and the underlying message. When you and the parents come from different cultures or backgrounds, it's easy to misunderstand and to be misunderstood. Here, too, you need to be a detective. Ryan's father, who objects when you prohibit Ryan from hitting, may be saying that he wants Ryan to be able to defend himself. Perhaps he was bullied as a child.

Swing Your Partner

Establishing a partnership begins as soon as parents set foot in the door. Make time to sit down and talk with them right away.

- Ask them about their goals and expectations for their child.

- Tell them about the centre's philosophy.

- Respect their culture. Ask about their routines, customs and expectations and adapt your program if possible.

- Give them information about child development whenever you can.

- Greet them when they bring or collect their children, and give them feedback about the day.

- Send home notes and newsletters.

- Plan parent-teacher meetings and special parent evenings.

- Make a special effort with parents whose values are different from yours. Research shows that they are less likely to consider the program as a source of information and support, and they may be the very ones who most need your help.[108]

Over time, these contacts provide rich soil for growing trust.

Some parents may already be working with specialists and parent groups and know an enormous amount about appropriate methods for managing the child's problems. Take the opportunity to learn as much from them as you can.[109]

The key is to find common ground. Review the parents' goals for the child, and look for solutions that satisfy everyone. Then schedule another meeting to assess the child's progress. You may have to meet several times to resolve the problem.

If you suspect the parents will punish the child when they get home, it may be best to address this issue directly. Tell them that you're informing them about the problem because it's important for them to know, the same way that it's important for them to know about the child's successes. But it is not necessary for them to do anything about it: you have already dealt with it appropriately at the program.

What if the child needs more help?

At a certain point you may want to suggest that the family get outside help for the child. This conversation will require the most extraordinary delicacy. Don't try to impose your values, and be sure to separate the child from the behaviour. Let Ian's parents know that you still have some concerns about Ian's behaviour. Be specific as you describe it: he bit Carol on Monday, spit at James on Tuesday, pushed Rutvi on Wednesday. Remind them that caring for Ian is a team effort, and tell them again how much you appreciate what they're doing. Outline the strategies you've tried, and explain that it is important for Ian's long-term development to get help for him.

If you think he might have a medical problem like a hearing loss, recommend that he see their pediatrician or family physician. But for other problems he may be better off at the local hospital's developmental clinic or a community agency that can call on a range of specialists. A trusted psychologist or psychiatrist is another possibility. Because the parents must make their own appointment, be sure to explain how the system works and provide a list of names and numbers that you have checked out ahead of time.

It is possible that the parents will reject the idea of outside intervention. This is their right, and their decision doesn't imply that they don't love their child — only that they aren't ready or that their view of the situation is different from yours.

How do I handle challenging behaviour when the parent is present?

When parent and caregiver are in the same room — as in a family resource program or a cooperative preschool or when the parent is picking up or delivering the child — everyone gets slightly confused about who's in charge.

Probably the best procedure is to hesitate for a moment to see if the parent will step in. But don't wait too long. If she doesn't act, use the chance to model appropriate behaviour. If she takes over, you will have a golden opportunity to see her interact with her child — and no matter what you think of this interaction, you'll have to let it go. You simply cannot criticize her in front of the child and other parents. If necessary, you can do some damage control and say the things you know the child needs to hear. Later create a private moment with the parent and tell her what you see, what you do, how the child responds. Remember to phrase the message so that she knows what to do rather than what not to do.

What should I say to the parents of the other children?

Whenever a child in your care has been hurt by another child and requires treatment, you must tell your supervisor and complete an incident report right away.

As soon as the parents of the injured child arrive, give them a copy of the report and let them know exactly what happened. Be prepared for an angry reaction, either on the spot or after they've seen the bruise. They may accuse you of not watching or demand that the other child leave the program, and they may not hear any explanation you offer. Just stay as calm and understanding as you can. In a day or two either you or the supervisor can talk to them privately about the plans for handling the situation. Even the parents of children who aren't directly involved may become upset, protest, gossip, contact the program's board of directors. Some may instruct their children not to play with the child with aggressive behaviour. Explain that you are watching carefully, keeping everyone safe and teaching the children to defend themselves with words — a skill they will need in the school playground in a year or two.

If parents want more information or wish to discuss a child who isn't theirs, refer them to the supervisor. Even though the children tell their parents what's going on, it is important to protect everyone's privacy.

It is your ethical obligation to be discrete, even when you need to share your feelings with fellow staff members. Don't talk in public places or mention last names.

What about asking a child with challenging behaviour to leave the program?

It is only when a child becomes a real danger to himself or others — and when you have exhausted every technique that you and the experts can devise — that exclusion becomes thinkable. But there is an important consideration when it comes to this drastic decision. Attachment is critical in child development. You spend many hours a day with this child, and it's important for his long-term development (and particularly his ability to trust) for him to know that he can trust you, that you can take care of him and that he can't destroy you. Sending him away doesn't teach anything positive. Rather it is the ultimate destroyer of self-esteem because it says in neon lights, "I don't want you here," confirming the child's most negative self-image. Educators have a responsibility to teach every child in their group (and no child is truly unteachable).

You can handle this — have confidence in yourself

- View inappropriate behaviour as an opportunity to teach. That will help with everything you do.

- Take it slowly, one behaviour at a time, one child at a time. Build in success by setting realistic goals.

- At the end of the day, reflect on what went wrong and what went right. Make notes in your agenda or on post-its so you can figure out what to do next time.

- Train yourself to look for, measure and record minute improvements. They are important signs of progress. Remember that the challenging behaviour has been etched in the brain over many months or years, and you can't eliminate it overnight.

- When you try a new approach, things may get worse before they get better. But if you don't see gains within a reasonable time, try another tack.

- If you work with other people, set common goals. Laugh, support and compliment each other. If you work alone, seek out your peers. Visit your neighborhood resource program, join a family day care agency or support group. Everyone needs someone to talk to.

- Give yourself a reward, not a guilt trip. Eat that ice cream, take that walk, rent that movie. Do whatever will keep you going.

Notes

1 R. E. Tremblay et al., "Predicting early onset of male antisocial behavior from preschool behavior," *Archives of General Psychiatry, 51* (1994): 733-734; J. Shamsie, *Troublesome Children: A Guide to Understanding and Managing Youth with Attention Deficit Hyperactivity Disorder, Oppositional Defiant Disorder and Conduct Disorder* (Etobicoke, ON: Institute for the Study of Antisocial Behaviour in Youth, 1995) 3.

2 R. G. Slaby et al., *Early Violence Prevention: Tools for Teachers of Young Children* (Washington D. C.: National Association for the Education of Young Children, 1995) 1-4; L. D. Eron and R. G. Slaby, "Introduction," in L. D. Eron J. H. Gentry and P. Schlegel, eds., *Reason to Hope: A Psychosocial Perspective on Violence & Youth* (Washington D.C.: American Psychological Association, 1994) 1.

3 Slaby et al. 3-4.

4 L. K. Chandler and C. M. Dahlquist, "Confronting the challenge: Using team-based functional assessment and effective intervention strategies to reduce and prevent challenging behaviour in young children," workshop presented at SpeciaLink Institute on Children's Challenging Behaviours in Child Care, Sydney, N.S., April 26-27, 1997; J. Ritchie and C. Pohl, "Rules of thumb workshop," *The Early Childhood Educator, 10* (Nov.-Dec. 1995): ll; C. S. Klass, K. A. Guskin and M. Thomas, "The early childhood program: Promoting children's development through and within relationships," *Zero to Three* (Oct.-Nov. 1995): 9.

5 F. Vitaro, M. De Civita and L. Pagani, "The impact of research-based prevention programs on children's disruptive behaviour," *Exceptionality Education Canada, 5* (1995): 106.

6 S. Landy and R. DeV. Peters, "Understanding and treating hyperaggressive toddlers," *Zero to Three* (Feb. 1991): 24.

7 R. E. Tremblay et al., "Do children in Canada become more aggressive as they approach adolescence?" in *Growing Up in Canada: National Longitudinal Survey of Children and Youth* (Ottawa: Human Resources Development Canada and Statistics Canada, 1996) 129-130.

8 Landy and Peters 24; R. E. Tremblay et al., "From childhood physical aggression to adolescent maladjustment: the Montreal prevention experiment," in R. DeV. Peters and R. J. McMahon, eds., *Preventing Childhood Disorders, Substance Abuse, and Delinquency* (Thousand Oaks, CA: Sage Publications, 1996) 271.

9 N. R. Crick, J. R. Cases and M. Mosher, "Relational and overt aggression in preschoolers," *Developmental Psychology, 33* (1997): 579-588.

10 P. Brennan, S. Mednick and E. Kandal, "Congenital determinants of violent and property offending," in D. J. Pepler and K. H. Rubin, eds., *The Development and Treatment of Childhood Aggression* (Hillsdale, NJ: Lawrence Erlbaum Associates, 1991) 87-90; A. J. Reiss, Jr. and J. A. Roth, eds., *Understanding and Preventing Violence* (Washington D.C.: National Academy Press, 1993) 364-365.

11 M. Leslie and G. DeMarchi, "Understanding the needs of substance-involved families and children in a child care setting," *Ideas, 3* (Dec. 1996): 12-16; R. Shore, *Rethinking the Brain: New Insights into Early Development* (New York: Families and Work Institute, 1997) 43-46; M. R. Burch, "Behavioral treatment of drug-exposed infants," *Children Today, 21* (1992): 12-14.

12 S. B. Campbell, *Behavior Problems in Preschool Children* (New York: Guilford Press, 1990) 50.

13 A. J. Ayres, *Sensory Integration and the Child* (Los Angeles: Western Psychological Services, 1979) 8, 56.

14 Shamsie 5-9.

15 Shamsie 8; D. K. Sherman, G. I. William and M. K. McGue, "Attention-deficit hyperactivity disorder dimensions: A twin study of inattention and impulsivity-hyperactivity," *Journal of the American Academy of Child and Adolescent Psychiatry, 36* (1997): 745-753; F. Levy et al., "Attention-deficit hyperactivity disorder: A category or a continuum? Genetic analysis of a large-scale twin study," *Journal of the American Academy of Child and Adolescent Psychiatry, 36* (1997): 737-744.

16 Shamsie 8; R. A. Barkley, *ADHD and the Nature of Self-Control* (New York: Guilford Press, 1997) 11.

17 S. Chess and A. Thomas, "Temperament and its functional significance," in S. I. Greenspan and G. H. Pollock, eds., *The Course of Life, Vol. II, Early Childhood* (Madison, CT: International Universities Press, 1989) 163-227.

18 Tremblay et al., *Growing Up in Canada* 129-130.

19 D. J. Pepler and R. G. Slaby, "Theoretical and developmental perspectives on youth and violence," in Eron et al. 48.

20 National Crime Prevention Council Canada, *Preventing Crime by Investing in Families* (Ottawa, 1996) 9-10; Shore 47-49.

21 Tremblay et al., *Growing Up in Canada* 130-131.

22 Slaby et al. 8; National Crime Prevention Council 29.

23 J. D. Coie, "Prevention of violence and antisocial behavior," in Peters and McMahon 6; L. D. Eron, L. R. Huesmann and A. Zelli, "The role of parental variables in the learning of aggression," in Pepler and Rubin 169-170; J. Haapasalo and R. E. Tremblay, "Physically aggressive boys from ages 6 to 12: Family background, parenting behavior, and prediction of delinquency," *Journal of Consulting and Clinical Psychology, 62* (1994): 1044-1052.

24 E. Donnerstein, R. G. Slaby and L. D. Eron, "The mass media and youth aggression," in Eron et al. 219-250.

25 B. Kaiser and J. S. Rasminsky, *The Daycare Handbook: A Parents' Guide to Finding and Keeping Quality Daycare in Canada* (Toronto: Little, Brown & Co., 1991); Canadian Child Care Federation, *National Statement on Quality Child Care* (Ottawa: author, 1994).

26 S. Turecki and L. T. Tonner, *The Difficult Child* (New York: Bantam Books, 1989); M. S. Kurcinka, *Raising Your Spirited Child* (New York: Harper Perennial, 1992).

27 R. E. Tremblay, "Early identification and intervention," presented at Dealing with Violence in Children and Youth Conference, Hamilton, ON, May 8, 1997; Coie in Peters and McMahon 6;

A. K. Kazdin, "Interventions for aggressive and antisocial children," in Eron et al. 346; Haapasalo and Tremblay 1044-1052.

28 T. Hay, "The case against punishment," *IMPrint* (Winter 1994-95): 10-11.

29 National Crime Prevention Council 10; E. E. Werner and R. S. Smith, *Overcoming the Odds: High Risk Children from Birth to Adulthood* (Ithaca: Cornell University Press, 1992).

30 Tremblay et al., "Predicting early onset" 733; Reiss and Roth 358; Coie in Peters and McMahon 6.

31 Tremblay, "Early identification and intervention."

32 K. A. Dodge, "Social cognition and children's aggressive behaviour," *Child Development, 51* (1980): 162-170; K. A. Dodge and C. L. Frame, "Social cognitive biases and deficits in aggressive boys," *Child Development, 53* (1982): 620-635.

33 A. E. Kazdin, "Treatment of antisocial behavior in children: Current status and future directions," *Psychological Bulletin, 102* (1987): 189; D. J. Pepler and K. H. Rubin, "Current challenges in the development and treatment of childhood aggression," in Pepler and Rubin xv.

34 National Crime Prevention Council 30-31.

35 National Crime Prevention Council 29; L. A. Serbin et al., "Aggressive, withdrawn, and aggressive/withdrawn children in adolescence: Into the next generation," in Pepler and Rubin 64-66; R. E. Tremblay, "Aggression, prosocial behavior, and gender," in Pepler and Rubin 75-76.

36 Shore 17, 20.

37 Shore 36.

38 Shore 40-41; *The First Years Last Forever: The New Brain Research and Your Child's Healthy Development* (Ottawa: Canadian Institute of Child Health, [1997]) 1-2.

39 Shore x, xii.

40 Coie 1-18.

41 Slaby et al. 2-4; National Crime Prevention Council 6, 10-11; Tremblay et al. in Peters and McMahon 292-293.

42 Tremblay et al. in Peters and McMahon 292-293; J. E. Dumas, "Treating antisocial behaviour in children: Child and family approaches," *Clinical Psychology Review, 9* (1989): 216.

43 Slaby 98; F. Vitaro and R. E. Tremblay, "Impact of a prevention program on aggressive children's friendships and social adjustment," *Journal of Abnormal Child Psychology, 22* (1994): 463.

44 Klass et al. 9.

45 M. Marion, "Guiding young children's understanding and management of anger," *Young Children* (Nov. 1997): 65; D. Gartrell, "Beyond discipline to guidance," *Young Children* (Sept. 1997): 41; E. Furman, *What Nursery School Teachers Ask Us About: Psychoanalytic Consultations in Preschools* (Madison, CT: International Universities Press, 1986) 81.

46 Shore 20.

47 Slaby et al. 28.

48 Slaby et al. 24.

49 C. Smith and C. Gay, "Early childhood social integration: Making friends," workshop presented at SpecialLink Institute on Children's Challenging Behaviours.

50 Slaby et al. 26, 36-37.

51 Klass 14.

52 Gartrell 41.

53 S. Mulligan et al., "Guiding the behavior of young children," in *The Child Care plus+ Curriculum on Inclusion: Practical Strategies for Early Childhood Programs* (Missoula, MT: Rural Institute on Disabilities/University of Montana, 1998) 13.

54 Mulligan et al. 17.

55 Slaby et al., 98-100; Tremblay, "Early identification and intervention."

56 *The Birth Order Book: Why You Are the Way You Are* (New York: Bantam-Dell Publishing Group, 1992).

57 E. Chornoboy and L. Keffer, "Working effectively with violent and aggressive students," workshop sponsored by Quebec Association for Preschool Professional Development, Montreal, Oct. 24-26, 1996. Pages 21-22 are based on WEVAS.

58 J. L. Anderson et al., "Issues in providing training to achieve comprehensive behavior support," in J. Reichle and D. P. Wacker, eds., *Communicative Alternatives to Challenging Behavior: Integrating Assessment and Intervention Strategies* (Baltimore: Paul H. Brookes Publishing, 1993) 375.

59 D. Creighton, interview, Vancouver, BC, May 9, 1996.

60 V. M. Durand, *Severe Behavior Problems: A Functional Communication Training Approach* (New York: Guilford Press, 1990) 19-20.

61 M. M. Quinn et al., *Addressing Student Problem Behavior: An IEP Team's Functional Behavior Assessment and Behavior Intervention Plans* (Washington D.C.: Center for Effective Collaboration and Practice, 1998) 1-2; "IDEA amendments of 1997 training package" (Washington D.C., National Information Center for Children and Youth with Disabilities, United States Department of Education Office of Special Education Programs, and Federal Resource Center for Special Education), module 10.

62 Chandler and Dahlquist; A. C. Repp et al., "Hypothesis-based interventions: A theory of clinical decision-making," in W. O'Donohue and L. Krasner, eds., *Theories of Behavior Therapy: Exploring Behavior Change* (Washington D.C.: American Psychological Association, 1995) 586; R. E. O'Neill et al., *Functional Assessment and Program Development for Problem Behavior: A Practical Handbook* (Pacific Grove, CA: Brooks/Cole Publishing, 1997) 2.

63 Durand 40.

64 B. A. Iwata et al., "Toward a functional analysis of self-injury," *Analysis and Intervention in*

Developmental Disabilities, 2 (1982): 3-20; G. Dunlap and L. Kern, "Assessment and intervention for children within the instructional curriculum," in Reichle and Wacker 182; O'Neill et al. 3, 8, 21.

65 S. W. Bijou, R. F. Peterson and M. H. Ault, "A method to integrate descriptive and experimental field studies at the level of data and empirical concepts," *Journal of Applied Behavior Analysis, 1* (1968): 175-191.

66 O'Neill et al. 39.

67 Durand 10-19; Repp et al. in O'Donohue and Krasner 590.

68 Repp et al. in O'Donohue and Krasner 589, 591; Lalli and Goh in Reichle and Wacker 23; K. G. Karsh et al., "In vivo functional assessment and multi-element interventions for problem behavior of students with disabilities in classroom settings," *Journal of Behavioral Education, 5* (1995): 189-210; A. C. Repp, D. Felce and L. E. Barton, "Basing the treatment of stereotypic and self-injurious behaviors on hypotheses of their causes," *Journal of Applied Behavior Analysis, 21* (1988): 281-289.

69 Durand 41; Dunlap and Kern in Reichle and Wacker 187-188.

70 O'Neill et al. 10.

71 Dunlap and Kern in Reichle and Wacker 186-187; O'Neill et al. 12.

72 O'Neill et al. 10, 43; Dunlap and Kern in Reichle and Wacker 188; B. W. Iwata, T. R. Vollmer and J. H. Zarcone, "The experimental (functional) analysis of behavior disorders: Methodology, applications, and limitations," in A. C. Repp and N. N. Singh, eds., *Perspectives on the Use of Nonaversive and Aversive Interventions for Persons with Developmental Disabilities* (Sycamore, IL: Sycamore Publishing, 1990) 305.

73 O'Neill et al. 35.

74 Dunlap and Kern in Reichle and Wacker 182-188; Repp et al. in O'Donohue and Krasner 596.

75 O'Neill et al. 36; Durand 59; L. H. Meyer and I. M. Evans, "Meaningful outcomes in behavioral intervention: Evaluating positive approaches to the remediation of challenging behavior," in Reichle and Wacker 423.

76 Chandler and Dahlquist.

77 O'Neill et al. 36.

78 Dunlap and Kern in Reichle and Wacker 189; O'Neill et al. 46-55.

79 Quinn et al. 3-4.

80 O'Neill et al. 66-68.

81 O'Neill et al. 66-67.

82 O'Neill et al. 67; F. C. Mace and M. L. Roberts, "Factors affecting selection of behavior interventions," in Reichle and Wacker 121-122.

83 Iwata et al. in Repp and Singh 318-320.

84 Repp et al. in O'Donohue and Krasner 600.

85 Durand 146-155; Mace and Roberts in Reichle and Wacker 120; O'Neill et al. 67.

86 Durand 151-152.

87 Durand 152-153; Mace and Roberts in Reichle and Wacker 120.

88 Meyer and Evans in Reichle and Wacker 407-428; Ron Schmidt, "Difficult social behavior problems: A consideration of behaviour teaching strategies," workshop presented at Early Childhood Educators of British Columbia Conference, Vancouver, May 10, 1996.

89 Slaby et al. 64-65.

90 Slaby et al. 64-65; Mulligan et al. 8-10.

91 L. Giuliani, "Anger and aggressivity in preschoolers," workshop presented at Centre de Psychoéducation, Montreal, QC, April 16, 1997; J. Milne-Smith, "Working with high needs children," workshop sponsored by Quebec Association for Preschool Professional Development, Montreal, Nov. 8, 1995.

92 Chandler and Dahlquist.

93 Dunlap and Kern in Reichle and Wacker 197.

94 The material on pages 29-30 is based on WEVAS.

95 Slaby et al. 73.

96 Slaby et al. 89.

97 Slaby et al. 90; D. Bonosew, interview, Montreal, QC, Jan. 10, 1997; Milne-Smith.

98 Slaby et al. 91; Gartrell 39; Chandler and Dahlquist; A. Kleinberg-Bassel, "Tools for crisis management," SpeciaLink Institute on Children's Challenging Behaviours.

99 Chornoboy and Keffer; Slaby et al. 90-91; E. F. Sussman, "Alternatives to time out," *Show 'N Tell Newsletter* (Summer 1994); Kleinberg-Bassel.

100 D. Jospe, "High needs children," course presented at Vanier College, Montreal, QC, Feb. 1-22, 1996.

101 Chornoboy and Keffer; Kleinberg-Bassel.

102 R. Spencler, personal communication, Sept. 8, 1998.

103 E. Chornoboy and L. Keffer, personal communication, Aug. 20, 1998.

104 Slaby et al. 94; Chornoboy and Keffer, WEVAS; Kleinberg-Bassel.

105 Slaby et al. 3.

106 Adapted from Slaby et al. 131.

107 Much of this section is based on an interview with A. Kleinberg-Bassel, Montreal, QC, July 24, 1998.

108 F. Bowden, *Supported Child Care: Enhancing Accessibility* (Victoria: British Columbia Ministry for Children and Families and Human Resources Development Canada, 1997) PR 25; Landy and Peters 27, 29; S. Kontos and W. Wells, "Attitudes of caregivers and the day care experiences of families," *Early Childhood Research Quarterly* (Mar. 1986): 47-67.

109 K. Andersen, interview, Vancouver, BC, May 12, 1996.

Resources

Behavior - Development - Individuality: A Newsletter about Caring for the High Maintenance Child. Available only on-line; www.temperament.com

Canadian Centre on Substance Abuse, FAS/FAE Information Service, 75 Albert St., Suite 300, Ottawa, ON K1P 5E7; 1-800-559-4514 or 613-235-4048; fax 613-235-8101; www.ccsa.ca/fasgen.htm

Carey, W. B. and S. C. McDevitt, *Coping with Children's Temperament: A Guide for Professionals* (New York: Harper Collins, 1995).

Essa, E., *A Practical Guide to Solving Preschool Behavior Problems* (New York, Delmar, 1998).

Fields, M. V. and C. Boesser, *Constructive Guidance and Discipline: Preschool and Primary Education* (Upper Saddle River, NJ: Prentice-Hall, 1998).

Flick, G. L., *ADD/ADHD Behavior-Change Resource Kit: Ready-to-Use Strategies and Activities for Helping Children with ADD* (West Nyack, NY: Center for Applied Research in Education, 1998).

Greene, R. W., *The Explosive Child: A New Approach for Understanding and Parenting Easily Frustrated, "Chronically Inflexible" Children* (New York: Harper Collins, 1998).

Greenspan, S. I. and J. Salmon, *The Challenging Child: Understanding, Raising and Enjoying the Five "Difficult" Types of Children* (Reading, PA: Addison Wesley, 1995).

Hallowell, E. M. and J. J. Ratey, *Driven to Distraction: Recognizing and Coping with Attention Deficit Disorder from Childhood through Adulthood* (New York: Simon and Schuster, 1994).

Irwin, S.H., ed., *Challenging the Challenging Behaviours: A Sourcebook Based on the SpeciaLink Institute on Challenging Behaviours in Child Care* (Wreck Cove, NS.: Breton Books, 1999).

Katz, L. G. and D. M. McClellan, *Fostering Children's Social Competence: The Teacher's Role* (Washington D.C.: National Association for the Education of Young Children, 1997).

Kleinfeld, J. and S. Wescott, eds., *Fantastic Antone Succeeds! Experiences in Educating Children with Fetal Alcohol Syndrome* (Fairbanks: University of Alaska, 1993). Available from BC FAS/E Support Network, 604-589-1854; fax 604-589-8438; E-mail fasnet@istar.ca

Kreidler, W. J. and S. T. Whittall, *Early Childhood Adventures in Peacemaking: A Conflict Resolution Activity Guide for Early Childhood Educators* (Cambridge, MA: Educators for Social Responsibility, 1999).

Kurcinka, M. S., *Raising Your Spirited Child* (New York: Harper Perennial, 1992).

LaForge, A. E., *Tantrums: Secrets to Calming the Storm* (New York: Pocket Books, 1996).

Levin, D. E., *Teaching Young Children in Violent Times: Building a Peaceable Classroom* (Cambridge, MA: Educators for Social Responsibility, 1994).

Making Friends. A series of four video programs. Image Media, #3-8755 Ash Street, Vancouver, BC V6P 6T3; 1-800-667-1500; fax 604-324-4855.

McCreight, B., *Recognizing and Managing Children with Fetal Alcohol Syndrome/Fetal Alcohol Effects: A Guide Book* (Washington D.C.: CWLA press, 1977).

McGinnis, E. and A. P. Goldstein, *Skill Streaming in Early Childhood: Teaching Prosocial Skills to the Preschool and Kindergarten Child* (Champaign, IL: Research Press, 1990).

National Clearinghouse on Family Violence, Health Promotion and Programs Branch, Health Canada, Ottawa, ON K1A 1B4; 1-800-267-1291 or 613-957-2938; fax 613-941-8930; www.hc-sc.gc.ca/hppb/familyviolence

National Crime Prevention Council, *Preventing Crime by Investing in Families: An Integrated Approach to Promote Positive Outcomes in Children* (Ottawa: author, 1996).

National Crime Prevention Council, *Risks or Threats to Children* (Ottawa: author, 1995).

O'Neill, R. E. et al., *Functional Assessment and Program Development for Problem Behavior: A Practical Handbook* (Pacific Grove, CA: Brooks/Cole, 1997).

Parry, A. et al., *Choosing Non-Violence: The Rainbow House Handbook to a Violence-Free Future for Young Children* (Chicago: Rainbow House/Arco Iris, 1990).

Quinn, M. M. et al., *Addressing Student Problem Behavior: An IEP Team's Functional Behavior Assessment and Behavior Intervention Plans* (Washington D.C.: Center for Effective Collaboration and Practice, 1998); www.air-dc.org/cecp/resources/problembehavior

Reynolds, E., *Guiding Young Children: A Child-Centered Approach* (Mountain View, CA: Mayfield, 1996).

Rodd, J., *Understanding Young Children's Behavior: A Guide for Early Childhood Professionals* (New York: Teachers College, 1996).

Second Step: A Violence Prevention Curriculum (Preschool-Kindergarten). Committee for Children, 2203 Airport Way South, Suite 500, Seattle, WA 98134-2027; 1-800-634-4449 or 206-343-1223.

Shore, R., *Rethinking the Brain: New Insights into Early Development* (New York: Families and Work Institute, 1997).

Slaby, R. G. et al., *Early Violence Prevention: Tools for Teachers of Young Children* (Washington D.C.: National Association for the Education of Young Children, 1995).

Turecki, S. and L. T. Tonner, *The Difficult Child* (New York: Bantam Books, 1989).

WEVAS (Working Effectively with Violent and Aggressive Students). Workshop information: 204-888-4759; E-mail spencler@mts.net

Wichert, S., *Keeping the Peace: Practicing Cooperation and Conflict Resolution with Preschoolers* (Philadelphia and Gabriola Island, BC: New Society, 1989).

Zirpoli, T. J. and K. J. Melloy, *Behavior Management: Applications for Teachers and Parents* (New York: Macmillan, 1993).

Functional Assessment Observation Form

Child's name _____ Date _____ Day of the week _____

Describe target behaviour(s) clearly and specifically _____

Appropriate ☐   Inappropriate ☐

Time	Activity	Behaviour What, where, how long, who else is involved	Antecedents What you were doing, what other children were doing (request, task, transition, no attention, peer interaction)	Consequences What you did and what other children did after the behaviour (redirect, obtain object, stop activity)	Setting events What happened before the antecedents (late arrival, noisy room, hungry)	Function What child got from the behaviour			
						Obtain	Avoid	Matro)less stimulation	Observer Initials

Adapted with permission from *Functional Assessment and Program Development for Problem Behavior: A Practical Handbook* by R.E. O'Neill, et al. (Pacific Grove, CA: Brooks/Cole Publishing, 1997).